750

SEEING IS BELIEVING

POEMS

NEW YORK

Charles Tomlinson

SEEING
IS BELIEVING

MCDOWELL, OBOLENSKY

Library of Congress Catalogue Card Number: 58-8704

First Printing

Acknowledgments are due to the editors of:

Essays in Criticism, The Hudson Review, Mandrake, The Paris Review, Poetry (Chicago), *The Sewanee Review, Shenandoah, The Spectator, Spectrum, Time and Tide.*

Manufactured in the United States of America by The Haddon Craftsmen, Scranton, Penna.

Designed by Kenneth Milford.

Contents

SEEING IS BELIEVING

The Atlantic

Launched into an opposing wind, hangs
   Grappled beneath the onrush,
And there, lifts, curling in spume,
   Unlocks, drops from that hold
Over and shoreward. The beach receives it,
   A whitening line, collapsing
Powdering-off down its broken length;
   Then, curded, shallow, heavy
With clustering bubbles, it nears
   In a slow sheet that must climb
Relinquishing its power, upward
   Across tilted sand. Unraveled now
And the shore, under its lucid pane,
   Clear to the sight, it is spent:
The sun rocks there, as the netted ripple
   Into whose skeins the motion threads it
Glances athwart a bed, honey-combed
   By heaving stones. Neither survives the instant
But is caught back, and leaves, like the after-image
   Released from the floor of a now different mind,
A quick gold, dyeing the uncovering beach
   With sunglaze. That which we were,
Confronted by all that we are not,
   Grasps in subservience its replenishment.

Beauty and the Beast

A SYMPHONIC METAMORPHOSIS

The glass is splintered in which Pico caught
Beauty. Only the Jesuit or the Irishman
Could piece those fragments: we lack
Both the mirror and the fable; poise, then,
Must be our shield, as when the flute
Suspended, dares the orchestral wave
And the beast, weary of gauds,
Scatters the mica lights in glittering showers
Out of its uncombed mane, rears
Sheer from its element to claw the mocker.
Apt as the dolphin, the spry tormentor
Cleaves through that clinging fury; with loving grasp
Unwinds its tentacles yet soothes them
As they slip. The beast licks the withdrawing hand
Scenting a favor, then rolls below
Back to its swaying lair. It snores.
A jewel glints beside that nostril.
It stretches. Hammocked in calm, its peace feeds
On its strength; it is content
To wander beyond itself, to mingle
A honied presence through the warm sea.
The sea sips it. Neither itself nor its opposite
It becomes a largeness
On which the flute-voice broods, hovers,
An invitation through which the dolphin slides
And plummets. Conceive that you are hung
Icarus-wise from where the voice has fled
Eying its metamorphosis that glides
A spiraling fish exploring somnolence.
All heaves with calm, calm which will rage
And under that stillness, seams of bedrock give

2

And the glass landscapes splinter, discompose.
Dolphin, that flute with wings, that
Flying fish, beauty is neither
Truth nor truth's reflection. It is the dance
The beast must lead
Who, dazzled by cymbal, bantered by reed and string,
Draws in cortège those fragile triumvirs.

Reflections

Like liquid shadows. The ice is thin
   Whose mirror smears them as it intercepts
Withdrawing colors; and where the crust,
   As if a skin livid with tautening scars,
Whitens, cracks, it steals from these deformations
   A style too tenuous for the image. A mirror lies, and
Flawed like this, may even lie with art,
   With reticence: "I exaggerate nothing,
For the reflections—scarcely half you see—
   Tell nothing of what you feel." Nature is blind
Like habit. Distrust them. We, since no mirrors,
   Are free both to question this deployment
And to arrange it—what we reflect
   Being what we choose. Though without deference,
We are grateful. When we perceive, as keen
   As the bridge itself, a bridge inlaying the darkness
Of smooth water, our delight acknowledges our debt—
   To nature, from whom we choose;
And, fencing that fullness back, to habit,
   The unsheathed image piercing our winter sleep.

Ponte Veneziano

TWO FIGURES

Tight-socketed in space, they watch
Drawn by a single glance,
Stripping the vista to its depth.

A prow pinpoints them:
They stare beyond it. The canopy
Which shades a boat
Flares from the line through which they gaze
Orange against coolness.

They do not see it, or,
Seeing, relegate the glow
To that point which it must occupy.

Undistracted, their glance channels itself
Ignoring the whiteness of a bridge
To cross beneath, where,
Closed by the vault,
It broods on the further light.

They do not exclaim,
But, bound to that distance,
Transmit without gesture
Their stillness into its ringed center.

Oxen: *Ploughing at Fiesole*

The heads, impenetrable
And the slow bulk
Soundless and stooping,
A white darkness—burdened
Only by sun, and not
By the matchwood yoke—
They groove in ease
The meadow through which they pace
Tractable. It is as if
Fresh from the escape,
They consent to submission,
The debris of captivity
Still clinging there
Unnoticed behind those backs:
"But we submit"—the tenor
Unambiguous in that stride
Of even confidence—
"Giving and not conceding
Your premises. Work
Is necessary, therefore—"
(With an unsevered motion
Holding the pauses
Between stride and stride)
"We will be useful
But we will not be swift: now
Follow us for your improvement
And at our pace." This calm
Bred from this strength, and the reality
Broaching no such discussion,
The man will follow, each
As the other's servant
Content to remain content.

6

The Mediterranean

I

In this country of grapes
Where the architecture
Plays musical interludes, flays
The emotions with the barest statement
Or, confusing the issue and the beholder,
Bewilders with an excessive formality,
There is also the sea.

II

               The sea
Whether it is "wrinkled" and "crawls"
Or pounds, plunders, rounding
On itself in thunderous showers, a
Broken, bellowing foam canopy
Rock-riven and driven wild
By its own formless griefs—the sea
Carries, midway, its burning stripe of light.

III

This country of grapes
Is a country, also, of trains, planes and gasworks.
"Tramway and palace" rankles. It is an idea
Neither the guidebook nor the imagination
Tolerates. The guidebook half lies
Of "twenty minutes in a comfortable bus"
Of "rows of cypresses, an
Uninterrupted series of matchless sights."
The imagination cannot lie. It bites brick;
Says: "This is steel—I will taste steel.

Bred on a lie, I am merely
Guidebooks, advertisements, politics."

The sea laps by the railroad tracks.
To have admitted this also defines the sea.

Distinctions

The seascape shifts

Between the minutest interstices of time
Blue is blue.

A pine-branch
Tugs at the eye: the eye
Returns to gray-blue, blue-black or indigo
Or it returns, simply,
To blue-after-the-pine-branch.

Here, there is no question of aberrations
Into pinks, golds or mauves:
This is the variation Pater indicated
But failed to prove.

Art exists at a remove.
Evocation, at two,
Discusses a blue that someone
Heard someone talking about.

Variant on a Scrap of Conversation

"There's nothing at all to be said for the day. . . ."

Except that through the wet panes
Objects arrange themselves,
Blue tessellations, faintly irised
Dividing the room
Into an observed music.

As one approaches the windows
Fugues of color
May be derived from a familiar interior,
A chair may be segmented and reassembled
In two steps.

To challenge the accepted vision
A further instance would be the wine-stopper,
Its head (cut into facets)
An eye for the cubist.

Icos

White, a shingled path
Climbs among dusted olives
To where at the hill-crest
Stare houses, whiter
Than either dust or shingle.
The view, held from this vantage
Unsoftened by distance, because
Scoured by a full light,
Draws lucid across its depth
The willing eye: a beach,
A surf-line, broken
Where reefs meet it, into the heaving
Blanched rims of bay-arcs;
Above, piercing the empty blue,
A gull would convey whiteness
Through the sole space which lacks it
But, there, scanning the shore,
Hangs only the eagle, depth
Measured within its level gaze.

Object in a Setting

I

From an empty sky
The morning deceives winter
With shadows and cold sapphire.

II

Astral, clear:
To wish it a more human image
Is to mistake its purpose.

Silent:
It is the marble city without trees.

Translucent, focal:
It is the city one may hold on the palm
Or lift, veined, against the sun.

Faceted, irised, burning:
It is the glass stair
To the hanging gardens.

III

The days turn to one their hard surfaces
Over which a glacial music
Pauses, renews, expands.

The Mausoleum

It is already six. From the steeple
  The even tones of a steady chime
Greet with their punctuality our lateness.
  The hall is shut. But one may
Visit the mausoleum in its now public grove
  Without cost or hindrance, and
With half as many steps as one would lose
  Were one to proceed. Here is the turning.

The trees thin and one sees its pyramid
  A steep roof tapering above stone steps.
Climb them. It is empty. The dead
  Have buried their dead and the living
Can approach it without fear and push open
  (As one may find it) the frayed door
To stand where a child might and where children do
  Play under the bare shelves of stone tiers.

We enter, the sunlight just about
  To fade on the wall and, from its glowing ground,
A blurred shadow detaches itself hovering
  And cannot decide whether a green or blue
Will the more grace its momentary existence
  Or whether a shot-red could invade
Decorously so impoverished a kingdom.

The light withdraws and the shadow softens
  Until it floats unnamably, gathered up
Into the colorless medium of early dusk:
  It is then that the eye, putting aside
Such distractions can move earnestly

Past the slung swag, chipped where it hangs
Under a white tablet, and slowly
    Climb upwards with its burden of questions.

For the tablet-square, remotely white
    But yellowed as if an effect of ivory
That has aged and which age has cracked,
    Proffers, scarified like the swag beneath it,
Unhealed wounds: ivory fractures
    But marble bruises, flakes and these dark
Incursions, heavy with shade, are the work
    Of hands, recording such meanings as you shall read.

Were I a guide you would vouchsafe my legend
    Of how a race halted in tumult here
To exorcise in such a wavering light
    The authority of death, and by left-hand magic
Practiced not against that but procreation,
    Signing each with his own name
Their composite work. But you must judge
    As you will and as the light permits.

For to grant to such fears their myth
    Is to distinguish them out of pity for a failing house.
Unleashed, it was no flickering colonnade
    Debouched this horde. The elegant swag
With the trim incision of the epitaphs no less
    Than the stone skull, mocked their impatience
And the blackened streets, the creeping architraves
    Of their Pandemonium, a city of mean years.

14

Swarming the base of the narrow walls
  As far as the raised arm can incise
Graffiti and beyond that as high as stone
  Can be aimed against stone in such a confine
The legend is complete however it is simple,
  Is plain, though under this dimmed
Clerestory the darkness liquefies it,
  And the work, however many the hands, one.

As surely as the air cooling and the scents
  That burn on the chillness at our exit,
The gravel rasping its trodden canon
  Under the weave of thought, usher us
Into that world to which this silence
  Scarred by so many hands is prologue,
You will concede that they have gained it whole
  Whatever they have lost in its possession.

Glass Grain

The glare goes down. The metal of a molten pane
Cast on the wall with red light burning through,
Holds in its firm, disordered square, the shifting strands
The glass conceals, till (splitting sun) it dances
Lanterns in lanes of light its own streaked image.
Like combed-down hair. Like weathered wood, where
Line, running with, crowds on line and swaying
Rounding each knot, yet still keeps keen
The perfect parallel. Like . . . in likes, what do we look for?
Distinctions? That, but not that in sum. Think of the fugue's
    theme:
After inversions and divisions, doors
That no keys can open, cornered conceits
Apprehensions, all ways of knowledge past,
Eden comes round again, the motive dips
Back to its shapely self, its naked nature
Clothed by comparison alone—related. We ask
No less, watching suggestions that a beam selects
From wood, from water, from a muslin-weave,
Swerving across our window, on our wall
(Transparency teased out) the grain of glass.

Tramontana at Lerici

Today, should you let fall a glass it would
  Disintegrate, played off with such keenness
Against the cold's resonance (the sounds
  Hard, separate and distinct, dropping away
In a diminishing cadence) that you might swear
  This was the imitation of glass falling.

Leaf-dapples sharpen. Emboldened by this clarity
  The minds of artificers would turn prismatic,
Running on lace perforated in crisp wafers
  That could cut like steel. Constitutions,
Drafted under this fecund chill, would be annulled
  For the strictness of their equity, the moderation of their pity.

At evening, one is alarmed by such definition
  In as many lost greens as one will give glances to recover,
As many again which the landscape
  Absorbing into the steady dusk, condenses
From aquamarine to that slow indigo-pitch
  Where the light and twilight abandon themselves.

And the chill grows. In this air
  Unfit for politicians and romantics
Dark hardens from blue, effacing the windows:
  A tangible block, it will be no accessory
To that which does not concern it. One is ignored
  By so much cold suspended in so much night.

Northern Spring

Nor is this the setting for extravagance. Trees
   Fight with the wind, the wind eludes them
Streaking its cross-lanes over the uneasy water
   Whose bronze whitens. To emulate such confusion
One must impoverish the resources of folly,
   But to taste it is medicinal. Consider

How through that broken calm, as the sun emerges,
   The sky flushes its blue, dyeing the grass
In the promise of a more stable tone:
   Less swift however than the cloud is wide—
Its shadow (already) quenching the verdure
   As its bulk muffles the sun—the blue drains
And the assault renews in colorless ripples.

Then, lit, the scene deepens. Where should one look
   In the profusion of possibilities? One conceives
Placing before them a square house
   Washed in the coolness of lime, a hub
For the scattered deployment, to define
   In pure white from its verdant ground
The variegated excess which threatens it.

Spring lours. Neither will the summer achieve
   That Roman season of an equable province
Where the sun is its own witness and the shadow
   Measures its ardor with the impartiality
Of the just. Evening, debauching this sky, asks
   To be appraised and to be withstood.

18

On a Landscape by Li Ch'eng

Look down. There is snow.
Where the snow ends
Sea, and where the sea enters
Gray among capes
Like an unvaried sky, lapping
From finger to finger
Of a raised hand, travelers
Skirt between snow and sea.
Minute, furtive and exposed,
Their solitude is unchosen and will end
In comity, in talk
So seasoned by these extremes
It will recall stored fruits
Bitten by a winter fire.
The title, without disapprobation,
Says "Merchants."

The Crane

That insect, without antennae, over its
Cotton-spool lip, letting
An almost invisible tenuity
Of steel cable, drop
Some seventy feet, with the
Grappling hook hidden also
Behind a dense foreground
Among which it is fumbling, and
Over which, mantis-like
It is begging or threatening, gracile
From a clear sky—that paternal
Constructive insect, without antennae,
Would seem to assure us that
"The future is safe, because
It is in my hands." And we do not
Doubt this veracity, we can only
Fear it—as many of us
As pause here to remark
Such silent solicitude
For lifting intangible weights
Into real walls.

Paring the Apple

There are portraits and still-lifes.

And there is paring the apple.

And then? Paring it slowly,
From under cool-yellow
Cold-white emerging. And . . . ?

The spring of concentric peel
Unwinding off white,
The blade hidden, dividing.

There are portraits and still-lifes
And the first, because "human"
Does not excel the second, and
Neither is less weighted
With a human gesture, than paring the apple
With a human stillness.

The cool blade
Severs between coolness, apple-rind
Compelling a recognition.

More Foreign Cities

"NOBODY WANTS ANY MORE POEMS ABOUT FOREIGN CITIES. . . ."
(From a recent disquisition on poetics).

Not forgetting Ko-jen, that
Musical city (it has
Few buildings and annexes
Space by combating silence),
There is Fiordiligi, its sun-changes
Against walls of transparent stone
Unsettling all preconception—a city
For architects (they are taught
By casting their nets
Into those moving shoals); and there is
Kairouan, whose lit space
So slides into and fits
The stone masses, one would doubt
Which was the more solid
Unless, folding back
Gold segments out of the white
Pith globe of a quartered orange,
One may learn perhaps
To read such perspectives. At Luna
There is a city of bridges, where
Even the inhabitants are mindful
Of a shared privilege: a bridge
Does not exist for its own sake.
It commands vacancy.

The Jam Trap

Wings filmed, the threads of knowledge thicken
Corded with mire. Bodies immerse
Slackly in sweetness. Sweetness is not satisfaction
Nor was the elation of the pursuit
The measure of its end. Aromas and inclinations
Delectable essences, and now
The inextricable gesture, sounds
Which communicate nothing, their sole speech
A scurrying murmur, each to himself his own
Monotone burden of discouragement. Preferring
The fed flock that, scattered, re-forms
Massed into echelon above copious fields,
The sky, their chosen element, has abandoned them.

Poem

Upended, it crouches on broken limbs
About to run forward. No longer threatened
But surprised into this vigilance
It gapes enmity from its hollowed core.

Moist woodflesh, softened to a paste
Of marl and white splinter, dangles
Where overhead the torn root
Casts up its wounds in a ragged orchis.

The seasons strip, but do not tame you.
I grant you become more smooth
As you are emptied and where the heart shreds
The gap mouths a more practiced silence.

You would impress, but merely startle. Your accomplice
Twilight is dragging its shadows here
Deliberate and unsocial: I leave you
To your own meaning, yourself alone.

A Meditation on John Constable

*"Painting is a science, and should be pursued as an inquiry into
the laws of nature. Why, then, may not landscape painting be
considered as a branch of natural philosophy, of which pictures
are but the experiments?"*

— JOHN CONSTABLE, *The History of Landscape Painting*

He replied to his own question, and with the unmannered
   Exactness of art; enriched his premises
By confirming his practice: the labor of observation
   In face of meteorological fact. Clouds
Followed by others, temper the sun in passing
   Over and off it. Massed darks
Blotting it back, scattered and mellowed shafts
   Break damply out of them, until the source
Unmasks, floods its retreating bank
   With raw fire. One perceives (though scarcely)
The remnant clouds trailing across it
   In rags, and thinned to a gauze.
But the next will dam it. They loom past
   And narrow its blaze. It shrinks to a crescent
Crushed out, a still lengthening ooze
   As the mass thickens, though cannot exclude
Its silvered-yellow. The eclipse is sudden,
   Seen first on the darkening grass, then complete
In a covered sky.
               Facts. And what are they?
He admired accidents, because governed by laws,
   Representing them (since the illusion was not his end)
As governed by feeling. The end is our approval
   Freely accorded, the illusion persuading us
That it exists as a human image. Caught
   By a wavering sun, or under a wind
Which moistening among the outlines of banked foliage

25

Prepares to dissolve them, it must grow constant;
Though there, ruffling and parted, the disturbed
  Trees let through the distance, like white fog
Into their broken ranks. It must persuade
  And with a constancy, not to be swept back
To reveal what it half-conceals. Art is itself
  Once we accept it. The day veers. He would have judged
Exactly in such a light, that strides down
  Over the quick stains of cloud-shadows
Expunged now, by its conflagration of color.
  A descriptive painter? If delight
Describes, which wrings from the brush
  The errors of a mind, so tempered,
It can forgo all pathos; for what he saw
  Discovered what he was, and the hand—unswayed
By the dictation of a single sense—
  Bodied the accurate and total knowledge
In a calligraphy of present pleasure. Art
  Is complete when it is human. It is human
Once the looped pigments, the pin-heads of light
  Securing space under their deft restrictions
Convince, as the index of a possible passion,
  As the adequate gauge, both of the passion
And its object. The artist lies
  For the improvement of truth. Believe him.

Frondes Agrestes

ON RE-READING RUSKIN

A leaf, catching the sun, transmits it:
"First a torch, then an emerald."

"Compact, like one of its own cones":
The round tree with the pyramid shadow.

First the felicities, then
The feelings to appraise them:

Light, being in its untempered state,
A rarity, we are (says the sage) meant
To enjoy "most probably" the effects of mist.

Nature's difficulties, her thought
Over dints and bosses, her attempts
To beautify with a leopard-skin of moss
The rocks she has already sculpted,
All disclose her purposes—the thrush's bill,
The shark's teeth, are not his story.

Sublimity is. One awaits its passing,
Organ voice dissolving among cloud rack.
The climber returns. He brings
Sword-shaped, its narrowing strip
Fluted and green, the single grass-blade, or
Gathered up into its own translucence
Where there is no shade save color, the unsymbolic rose.

Geneva Restored

"The secreted city . . ."—F. T. PRINCE.

Limestone, faulted with marble; the lengthening swell
Under the terraces, the farms in miniature, until
With its sheer, last leap, the Salève becomes
The Salève, juts naked, the cliff which nobody sees
Because it pretends to be nothing, and has shaken off
Its seashore litter of house-dots. Beneath that,
This—compact, as the other is sudden, and with an inaccessible
Family dignity: close roofs on a gravel height,
Building knit into rock; the bird's nest of a place
Rich in protestant pieties, in heroic half-truths
That was Ruskin's. Guard and rebuild it. We are in the time
(The eternity rather) before the esplanades, New York
Bear-ridden and the casino unbuilt, Paris and London
Remain at Paris and London, and four miles square
A canton of resined air that will not be six
Refreshes a sociality that will not be pent
In the actual. Round this inconceivable
Point of patience, men travel on foot.

Farewell to Van Gogh

The quiet deepens. You will not persuade
   One leaf of the accomplished, steady, darkening
Chestnut-tower to displace itself
   With more of violence than the air supplies
When, gathering dusk, the pond brims evenly
   And we must be content with stillness.

Unhastening, daylight withdraws from us its shapes
   Into their central calm. Stone by stone
Your rhetoric is dispersed until the earth
   Becomes once more the earth, the leaves
A sharp partition against cooling blue.

Farewell, and for your instructive frenzy
   Gratitude. The world does not end tonight
And the fruit that we shall pick tomorrow
   Await us, weighing the unstripped bough.

Cézanne at Aix

And the mountain: each day
Immobile like fruit. Unlike, also
—Because irreducible, because
Neither a component of the delicious
And therefore questionable,
Nor distracted (as the sitter)
By his own pose and, therefore,
Doubly to be questioned: it is not
Posed. It is. Untaught
Unalterable, a stone bridgehead
To that which is tangible
Because unfelt before. There
In its weathered weight
Its silence silences, a presence
Which does not present itself.

In Defense of Metaphysics

Place is the focus. What is the language
Of stones? I do not mean
As emblems of patience, philosophers' hopes
Or as the astrological tangents
One may assemble, draw out subjectively
From a lapidary inertia. Only we
Are inert. Stones act, like pictures, by remaining
Always the same, unmoving, waiting on presence
Unpredictable in absence, inhuman
In a human dependence, a physical
Point of contact, for a movement not physical
And on a track of force, the milestone
Between two infinities. Stones are like deaths.
They uncover limits.

Reeds

The blades sway. They ride
Unbleached, tugged in their full sap
By the slow current. Hindering
From thought, they think us back
To that first green, which the mind
Tender-skinned, since grazed to the pain of sight,
Shrank at, lapping us in a half-green content
And, there, left us. By nature
Trenchant, blue double-whets them,
Burned through the water from a sky
That has long looked at it
Untempered by any mist. In this
There is of theme or apophthegm
No more than meets the eye. The blades sway.

Night-Piece: The Near and the Far

Declivities, striations, ledge over ledge of mounting
Cloud. A solid smoke, unsifted before the wind,
But shaped against it, crowded and blown together
From the horizon upwards. It goes on drifting, piling,
Rags into rock-ranks, mist to masses
Caught endlessly through the alien current, held
Riding the stream which buoys, then bloats, drags it
Into a further dark. Fissured, lit by the moon behind
Prizing from black an ore of undertones,
Over the houseless space, a hearth spills down.

On the Hall at Stowey

Walking by map, I chose unwonted ground,
   A crooked, questionable path which led
Beyond the margin, then delivered me
   At a turn. Red marl
Had rutted the aimless track
   That firmly withheld the recompense it hid
Till now, close by its end, the day's discoveries
   Began with the dimming night:

A house. The wall-stones, brown.
   The doubtful light, more of a mist than light
Floating at hedge-height through the sodden fields
   Had yielded, or a final glare
Burst there, rather, to concentrate
   Sharp saffron, as the ebbing year—
Or so it seemed, for the dye deepened—poured
   All of its yellow strength through the way I went:

Over grass, garden-space, over the grange
   That jutted beyond, lengthening-down
The house line, tall as it was,
   By tying it to the earth, trying its pride
(Which submitted) under a nest of barns,
   A walled weight of lesser encumbrances—
Few of which worsened it, and none
   As the iron sheds, sealing my own approach.

All stone. I had passed these last, unwarrantable
   Symbols of—no; let me define, rather
The thing they were not, all that we cannot be,
   By the description, simply of that which merits it:

Stone. Why must (as it does at each turn)
    Each day, the mean rob us of patience, distract us
Before even its opposite?—before stone, which
    Cut, piled, mortared, is patience's presence.

The land farmed, the house was neglected: but
    Gashed panes (and there were many) still showed
Into the pride of that presence. I had reached
    Unchallenged, within feet of the door
Ill-painted, but at no distant date—the least
    Our prodigal time could grudge it; paused
To measure the love, to assess its object,
    That trusts for continuance to the mason's hand.

Five centuries—here were (at the least) five—
    In linked love, eager excrescence
Where the door, arched, crowned with acanthus,
    Aimed at a civil elegance, but hit
This sturdier compromise, neither Greek, Gothic
    Nor Strawberry, clumped from the arching-point
And swathing down, like a fist of wheat,
    The unconscious emblem for the house's worth.

Conclusion surrounded it, and the accumulation
    After Lammas growth. Still coming on
Hart's-tongue by maiden-hair
    Thickened beneath the hedges, the corn leveled
And carried, long-since; but the earth
    (Its tint glowed in the house wall)
Out of the reddish dark still thrust up foison
    Through the browning-back of the exhausted year:

Thrust through the unweeded yard, where earth and house
    Debated the terrain. My eye
Caught in those flags a gravestone's fragment
    Set by a careful century. The washed inscription
Still keen, showed only a fragile stem
    A stave, a broken circlet, as
(Unintelligibly clear, craft in the sharp decrepitude)
    A pothook grooved its firm memorial.

Within, wet from the failing roof,
    Walls greened. Each hearth refitted
For a suburban whim, each room
    Denied what it was, diminished thus
To a barbarous mean, had comforted (but for a time)
    Its latest tenant. Angered, I turned to my path
Through the inhuman light, light that a fish might swim
    Stained by the grayness of the smoking fields.

Five centuries. And we? What we had not
    Made ugly, we had laid waste—
Left (I should say) the office to nature
    Whose blind battery, best fitted to perform it
Outdoes us, completes by persistence
    All that our negligence fails in. Saddened,
Yet angered beyond sadness, where the road
    Doubled upon itself I halted, for a moment
Facing the empty house and its laden barns.

Cradock Newton

FROM AN EPITAPH

"Gurney, Hampton, Cradock Newton, last
Held on the measure of that antient line
Of barons' blood . . ." Paused by whose tomb,
Ignorant of its bones I read the claim
(Lie, half-lie or three-quarters true): "He lov'd
To feed the poor." Tasting such phrases,
So I taste their plight, and pity them,
But seeing the angel with its scales of stone—
Who suffers (I ask in thought) the greater need
Now time has stripped them both—those nameless
Or these named? For pity is the most
That love dares plead from justice. And will the poor
Love Cradock Newton when he creeps unhoused,
Naked at last before the rich man's door?

The Castle

It is a real one—no more symbolic
Than you or I. There are no secrets
Concerning the castellan; in the afternoons
His hospitality labors for the satisfaction
Not of guests, but visitors; in the mornings
Directing his renovations, he sits alone;
A settled gloom is threaded by scavengers
Who, through the dust of galleries, down
Through those sadder reticulations from which the myths have
   faded,
Resurrect for the present as much of the improbable past
As it can tolerate. Dust is their element
But they finger the mysteries, as they unlink
The pendants of chandeliers into their winking suds:
He is easeless watching this progress, they
Sullen among their swaying burdens, remain
Unmindful of the minuter jealousies he would haunt them with
But which (since his power is nominal)
He must mute into reprimands, or twist, unnoticed
Round the stem of a candle-sconce, to suffer in person
Those daily burnishings under a menial hand.
He looks away. Townwards, below him
Where the sidings smoke, his glance struggles
Then settles. He has risen by the scale of talent
Into the seat of blood. But justice is less than just
And he is bored. His own master and his prisoner,
He serves a public. The soot sifts through
In flocculent grains and the clouds he watches
He now tastes. Whom does a public serve?
The smoke unwinds from its mounting coils,
Falling apart, a wavering drift

As the wind takes it. This morning blur
Conceals no innuendoes. A statement in prose,
It reserves on its neighboring hill
A last artifact which, dusted, is ready now
To receive the solemnity or the distraction
Of visitors. He rises to go down.
It is twelve, and conscience excuses him.

Civilities of Lamplight

Without excess (no galaxies
Gauds, illiterate exclamations)
It betokens haven,
An ordering, the darkness held
But not dismissed. One man
Alone with his single light
Wading obscurity refines the instance,
Hollows the hedge-bound track, a sealed
Furrow on dark, closing behind him.

The Request

Look from your stillness as the light resumes.
    From underneath your brim that, shading,
Sags like a burdock leaf, review
    Once more the accretions of moss
Graying the stones at the level of your eye.

Recover, rising, the ease in which you came
    Spreading on the grass your scarf and then yourself
Laid on its crimson that would have challenged
    Till you offset it, leaning there
With the unconscious rectitude of grace
    A little stiffly upon the elbow. Recall

Gradually the supple line
    With which your hand, composing the calm
You and your solitary companion share,
    Dipped, reiterated the brim in undulation,
Then subsided as you removed your elbow
    To slide instantly into that present shade.

She looks. And a flawed perfection
    Disburses her riches. She is watched
And knows she is watched. The crimson reveals itself
    Recommending her posture and assured by it
Both of her charm and her complicity: the error
    And the request were mine, the conclusion is yours.

Château de Muzot

Than a choice of subject,
Rather to be chosen by what has to be said
And to say it—by cold fire
Such as these walls withhold and the eye
Tactually commends, the light
Thereby assuring us of a mass
That we would wish to touch. From this
You cannot detract. It is beyond satire
And beyond you. A shriven self
Looks out at it. You cannot
Add to this. Footholds for foison
There are none. Across stoneface
Only the moss, flattened, tightly-rosetted
Which, ignorant of who gives
Accepts from all weathers
What it receives, possessed
By the nature of stone.

The Ruin

Dissolving, the coals shift. Rain swaddles us
  And the fire, driving its shadows through the room
Recalls us to our intention as the flames
  That, by turns, sink guttering or mount
To pour red light through every crater,
  Threaten the galleries of crumbling ash.

The ruins sag, then sift downwards,
  Their fall so soundless that, for the first time,
We distinguish the unbroken, muffled sibilance
  Rain has accompanied us with. Our talk
Recovers its theme—the ruin we should have visited
  Abandoned, now, in its own emptiness.

For the morning promised what, through the darkening air,
  Afternoon retracted, nor will the evening
Welcome us under its turmoil of wet leaves
  Where we have lost the keenness of such acridity
As a burnt ruin exhales long afterwards
  Into the coolness when rain has ceased.

It stands on the hill slope. Between green and green
  There is the boundary wall that circles
And now hides it. Within, one can see nothing
  Save the third, checkered indefinite green
Of treetops—until, skirting these limits
  One discovers, open upon the emptied confine, the gate.

For a week, the swift traffic of demolition
  That mottled with oil their stagnant rain,
Advanced through the deepening ruts,

Converged on the house, disjointed, reassembled
And carted, flung (what had sprawled unhinged)
   The door into the wreckage and burnt both.

The door which, though elegant, leaned from the true
   A little to one side, was shamed
By the nearby, slender but rigid elm—
   An unchanging comedy, varied
Only as the seasons thought fit and as the days
   Under their shifting lights reviewed it.

The house was not ancient, but old: deserted,
   The slewed door had focused its rotting style
And, as proportion tugged from decrepitude
   A faint self-respect, it was the door
With the firmness of an aged but practiced arbiter
   Bestowed it back over the entire ruin.

Impartial with imperfections, it could accuse
   By this scant presence its clustering neighbors
Gross with the poverty of utility. Thus challenging, it stayed,
   A problem for the authorities, a retreat for urchins
Until the urchins burnt half and the authorities
   Publicly accomplished what their ally had attempted by stealth.

There remains now the leveled parapet of earth,
   The bleak diagram of a foundation, a hearth
Focusing nothing and, cast into it, the filigree ghost
   Of an iron fanlight. Could we assemble
Beside its other fragments, that last grace
   Under this meaner roof, they would accuse us still—

44

And accusing, speak from beyond their dereliction
    Out of their life; as when a vase
Cracked into shards, would seem
    Baldly to confess, "Men were here,"
The arabesque reproves it, tracing in faint lines:
    "Ceremonies and order were here also."

Nor could we answer: our houses
    Are no longer ourselves; they dare not
Enter our hopes as the guests of meditation
    To reanimate, warmed by this contact,
The laric world where the bowl glistens with presence
    Gracing the table on which it unfolds itself.

Thus fire, renewed at our hearth, consumes.
    Yet it cannot create from the squalor of moderation
A more than fortuitous glory, multiplying its image
    Over the projections of lacquered wood. Charged with their
        past,
Those relics smolder before they are compounded
    And turned by the spade under a final neatness.

The window lightens. The shell parts
    Beyond between cloud and sky line.
Thunder-light, flushing the walls, yellows them
    Into a more ardent substance than their own
And can do no more. The effect is nature's
    Who ignores it, and in whose impoverishment we domicile.

ANTECEDENTS:

A Homage and Valediction

"Oh! que ses yeux ne parlent plus d'Idéal
Mais simplement d'humains échanges!"

"After such knowledge, what forgiveness?"

THE SCENE: chiefly the Paris of Jules Laforgue and
Stéphane Mallarmé.

I. Nothing: a Divagation

Not the calm—the clarity
After the storm. There are
In lucidity itself
Its crystal abysses
Perspective within perspective:
The white mind holds
An insufficiency, a style
To contain a solitude
And nothing more. Thus,
The infirm alchemy
Of platonic fantasy—
Word, the idea,
Spacing the vacuum: snow-prints
Wanting a direction; perhaps
At the most, as a constellation
The cut stone
Reassembled on dark.

II. Praeludium

"Je ne puis quitter ce ton: que d'échos. . . ."—Derniers Vers

The horn has sounded.

Sunsets! They are interminable. Too late, however
For his exclamations. Sunsets. . . . A point
Of interrogation, perhaps? How long
Can a sun go on setting? The thin refrain
Dies in a dying light as
"The splendor falls." And it continues
Falling flaking into the leaf-drift. First,
It was Byron; the laureate
Next remarked on the inveterate music
Microscopically, reserving his
Tintinnabulations (caught in the half-stopped ear)
For elegiacs between occasions, the slow sun
Maintaining its progress (downwards)
Chromatically lamented. "He is a master
Of miniature," said Nietzsche
Speaking from solitude
Into solitude—he was describing
The bayreuthian minotaur, lamenting the hecatombs,
Yet forced to concede
An undionysiac, unapollonian distinction
In that gamut of melancholias. "Art is a keyboard
For transitions," said Mallarmé: "between something and
    nothing."
The music persisted
"And when I heard it" (Charles Baudelaire, the
Slow horn pouring through dusk an orange twilight)
"I grew insatiate." We had our laureates, they
Their full orchestra and its various music. To that
                                                    Enter

On an ice-drift
A white bear, the grand Chancellor
From Analyse, uncertain
Of whom he should bow to, or whether
No one is present. It started with Byron, and
Liszt, says Heine, bowed to the ladies. But Jules . . . .
Outside,

De la musique avant toute chose
The thin horns gone glacial
And behind blinds, partitioning Paris
Into the rose-stained mist,
He bows to the looking-glass. Sunsets.

III. Lacunae

Autumn! Leaves in symphonic tumult,
Fall of Antigones and Philomelas
That my grave-digger (alas, poor Yorick!)
Must shift with his spade; and from the window
In the wet, all my chimneys
On the factories . . .

Chaplin, as Hamlet. A role we have yet to see
For the most part. As also
That spoiled Lutheran, masked
As his Zarathustra. Our innate
Perspicacity for the moderate
Is a national armory. "I have not
Read him; I have read about him":
In usum delphini—for the use
Of the common man. After Nietzsche
(Downwards) Sartre, after whom
Anouilh, dauphin's delight. And thus
Rimbaud the incendiary,
Gamin contemporary
With Gosse, the gentleman
Arrived late. He was dressed
In the skin of a Welsh lion, or the lion
Wore his—for the light
Was dubious, the marsh softening
And the company, willing to be led
Back to the forsaken garden by a route
Unfamiliar—yet as it wound
Dimly among the fetishes, a bewilderment
Of reminiscence. The force
That through the green dark, drove them

Muffled dissatisfactions. Last light, low among tempests
Of restless brass. Last music
For the sable throne (She comes, she comes!)
As the horns, one by one
Extinguish under the wave
Rising into the level darkness.
                              And Chaplin,
As Hamlet? That would have been
A more instructive frenzy. Eye-level light
Disclosing the field's wrinkles
Closes.

IV. Milieux

We lack nothing
But the milieu.
De la fumée avant toute chose
Weaving the smoke, subjective
Faun with a cigarette, Stéphane assembled one:
The page (the horns gone glacial)
Discovered its landscapes
As arctic gardens,
A luminous aura, hinting the penetration
Of green skeins, a snow-light
Bruising the mind.
There were divagations (platonic)
There were departures (actual)
And the predilection
For a confirmed madness
Confused them, one with another. Thus Missolonghi
Was re-enacted at Harrar
At Papeete, Atouana—"alone
And surrounded by verdure":
Preludes to Taos.
We lack nothing
But a significant sun.

V. The Bells: A Period Piece
"What a world of solemn thought. . . ."—POE.

Hygienic bells, pale
Galilean bells (O what a wealth
Of melody!)—the lingering
Aftertone of all that sullen, moneyed harmony
Drove, and will drive, before its tidal choir
The great departures and the soft refusals.

Expostulation with the deaf—impossible
"To modify this situation":
Rustle of lavender and thyme, clean collars
As the wind is gagged
Full of this crystalline confusion:

The sky, dressed in the sound of Sunday colors
The season (fall of Antigones and Philomelas!)
The trains (picturesque destinations!) missed
The girls (white as their prayer-books) are released,
Rustle in lavender and thyme
From incense back to houses where
Their white pianos cool each thirsty square.

Chimeric bells, provincial bells—
And from the rust within their throats (O what a world
Of solemn thought!) now silence breaks:
Secure no longer in their theme
Or violence of its repetitions,
The generations abdicate
To us the means to vacillate.

VI. Something: A Direction

Out of the shut cell of that solitude there is
   One egress, past point of interrogation.
Sun is, because it is not you; you are
   Since you are self, and self delimited
Regarding sun. It downs? I claim? Cannot
   Beyond such speech as this, gather conviction?
Judge, as you will, not what I say
   But what is, being said. It downs
Recovered, coverless, in a shriven light
   And you, returning, may to a shriven self
As from the scene, your self withdraws. You are downing
   Back from that autumn music of the light, which
Split by your need, to know the textures of your pain,
   Refuses them in your acceptance. You accept
An evening, washed of its overtones
   By strict seclusion, yet are not secluded
Withheld at your proper bounds. From there
   Your returns may enter, welcome strangers
Into a civil country (you were not the first
   To see it), but a country, natural and profuse
Unbroken by past incursions, as the theme
   Strung over stave, is rediscovered
After dismemberment in the canon, and over stave
   Can still proceed, unwound, unwinding
To its established presence, its territory
   Staked and sung; and the phrase descends
As a phase concluded. Released
   From knowing to acknowledgment, from prison
To powers, you are new-found
   Neighbored, having earned relation
With all that is other. Still you must wait,

56

For evening's ashen, like the slow fire
Withdrawn through the whitened log
  Glinting through grain marks where the wood splits:
Let be its being: the scene extends
  Not hope, but the urgency that hopes for means.

Notes to Antecedents

III. LACUNAE

"The force/ That through the green dark . . ."
                        (Cf. DYLAN THOMAS, Eighteen Poems).

IV. MILIEUX

Rimbaud departed to Harrar; Gaugin to Papeete and Atouana.
From Atouana the latter wrote: "You have no idea of the peace
in which I live here, entirely alone, surrounded by verdure."
(Quoted by R. H. WILENSKI, p. 177 Modern French Painters,
Faber 1944.)

V. THE BELLS

"Impossible de modifier cette situation." In rendering this from
Derniers Vers, one cannot avoid the tone of (early) Eliot because
Eliot himself has not avoided the tone of Laforgue.

The Churchyard Wall

Stone against stone, they are building back
    Round the steepled bulk, a wall
That enclosed from the neighboring road
    The silent community of graves. James Bridle,
Jonathan Silk and Adam Bliss, you are well housed
    Dead, howsoever you lived—such headstones
Lettered and scrolled, and such a wall
    To repel the wind. The channel, first,
Dug to contain a base in solid earth
    And filled with the weightier fragments. The propped yews
Will scarcely outlast it; for, breached,
    It may be rebuilt. The graves weather
And the stone skulls, more ruinous
    Than art had made them, fade by their broken scrolls.
It protects the dead. The living regard it
    Once it is falling, and for the rest
Accept it. Again, the ivy
    Will clasp it down, save for the buried base
And that, where the frost has cracked,
    Must be trimmed, reset, and across its course
The barrier raised. Now they no longer
    Prepare: they build, judged by the dead.
The shales must fit, the skins of the wall-face
    Flush, but the rising stones
Sloped to the center, balanced upon an incline.
    They work at ease, the shade drawn in
To the uncoped wall which casts it, unmindful
    For the moment, that they will be outlasted
By what they create, that their labor
    Must be undone. East and west
They cope it edgewise; to the south

Where the talkers sit, taking its sun
When the sun has left it, they have lain
The flat slabs that had fallen inwards
Mined by the ivy. They leave completed
Their intent and useful labors to be ignored,
To pass into common life, a particle
Of the unacknowledged sustenance of the eye,
Less serviceable than a house, but in a world of houses
A merciful structure. The wall awaits decay.

About the Author

Charles Tomlinson was born in Staffordshire, England, in 1927. He read English at Queens' College, Cambridge and has lived in Northern Italy and London. He now lives in Somerset with his wife and daughter and teaches at Bristol University. A volume of poetry, *The Necklace*, was published in England in 1955.

Tomlinson's work, both as poet and as critic, has appeared widely throughout the United States in, among others, the *Sewanee* and *Hudson* reviews, and during 1956 he was awarded the Hokin Prize for verse by *Poetry*.

Seeing Is Believing contains poems written over the past four years in which he has attempted to widen the ethical implications of his earlier verse. The extra-literary influences of which he has been most conscious are the cinema and visual arts. Writing of his own work in the *Poems in Folio* series, Tomlinson has commented: "The hardness of crystals, the facets of cut glass; but also the shifting of light, the energizing weather which is a result of the combination of sun and frost—these are the images for a certain mental climate, components for the moral landscape of my poetry in general."